HARNESSING ENERGY
• HARNESSING ENERGY •

HYDRO POWER

BY DIANE BAILEY

CREATIVE
PAPERBACKS

TABLE OF CONTENTS

PEACE AND WAR. WEALTH AND POVERTY. PROGRESS AND SETBACKS. HISTORY HAS BROUGHT HUGE SWINGS IN THE HUMAN CONDITION, AND WITH EVERY CHOICE PEOPLE MAKE, THERE IS THE POTENTIAL TO MOVE FORWARD OR STEP BACKWARD. AT THE CORE OF THIS CONTINUAL STRUGGLE HAS BEEN THE QUEST FOR ENERGY. ENERGY GAVE HUMANS POWER AND MOTIVATED THEM TO DO GREAT THINGS — WITH BOTH POSITIVE AND NEGATIVE EFFECTS. WITHOUT ENERGY, PEOPLE WOULD NOT BE ABLE TO DRIVE CARS, OPERATE COMPUTERS, OR POWER FACTORIES. WARS ARE FOUGHT TRYING TO DOMINATE SOURCES OF ENERGY. FORTUNES ARE MADE AND LOST DEPENDING ON HOW THAT ENERGY IS MANAGED. THE LAWS OF PHYSICS STATE THAT ENERGY CANNOT BE CREATED OR DESTROYED. THAT IS TRUE, BUT ENERGY CAN BE HARNESSED AND DIRECTED. IT CAN BE WASTED, OR IT CAN BE COAXED INTO EFFICIENCY. CIVILIZATIONS AND TECHNOLOGIES HAVE LEAPED FORWARD — AND SOMETIMES BACKWARD — AS HUMANS HAVE TAPPED INTO EARTH'S SOURCES OF ENERGY.

Dams harness water's massive force and play a key role in modern hydropower.

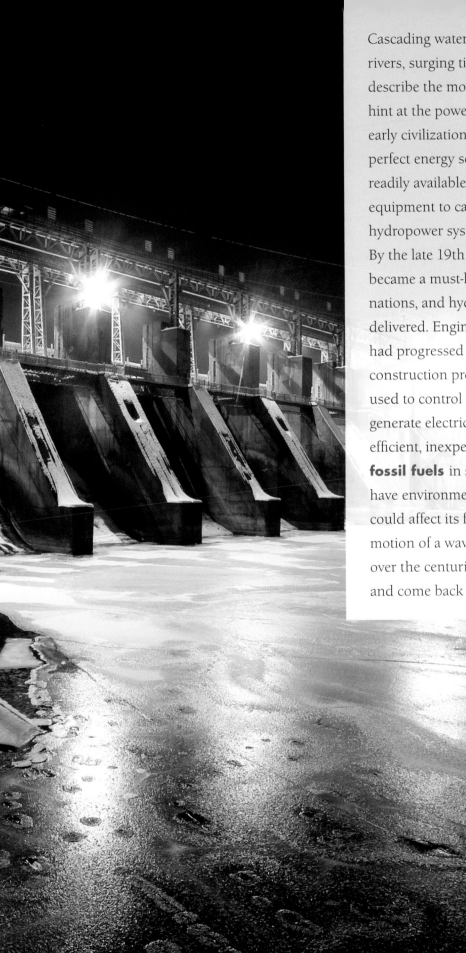

Cascading waterfalls, rushing rivers, surging tides: the words that describe the movement of water hint at the power it contains. For early civilizations, water was a nearly perfect energy source. It was free and readily available. It needed only simple equipment to capture its power. Early hydropower systems ran machinery. By the late 19th century, electricity became a must-have in developing nations, and hydropower once again delivered. Engineering technology had progressed enough that massive construction projects—dams—could be used to control the flow of water and generate electricity. Hydropower is efficient, inexpensive, and cleaner than **fossil fuels** in some ways, but it does have environmental drawbacks that could affect its future. Mimicking the motion of a wave, hydropower usage over the centuries has built, crashed, and come back again.

CHAPTER ONE

WHITE COAL

WATER, WATER EVERYWHERE. FOR PEOPLE IN ANCIENT TIMES, WATER WAS THE MOST BASIC MATERIAL AROUND. Some of it lay peacefully in ponds and lakes, but a lot of it did not. People could see water's strength in the splash of waves. They could hear it in the roar of a waterfall and feel it in the current of a river. Water held tremendous potential, if people could only use its power. Fortunately, all they needed was one of humanity's most basic inventions: the wheel.

Water covers about 70 percent of Earth's surface and is also found in the air and living things.

Located in Hama, Syria, the largest noria in existence has a wheel measuring 65.6 feet (20 m) across.

The ancient Egyptians used a kind of waterwheel called a noria. The outside edge of the wheel had buckets fastened to it, much like seats on a Ferris wheel. The wheel was placed halfway under water to catch the current. The current turned the wheel, and the buckets filled with water. As the buckets moved upward, they dumped their contents into a trough. From there, the water ran to fields to water crops.

In ancient Greece, large waterwheels were connected to smaller ones in a system of gears. This focused the energy in a single spot, providing enough power to move stones that could grind grain. The Romans later had access to this technology. However, one writer of the time reported that the technology was not widely used, probably because people depended on slaves to do their labor, rather than machines. However, during the High and Late Middle Ages in Europe, from about A.D. 1000 to 1500, slaves were less common. The waterwheel became much more important. One waterwheel could do the work of about 40 people.

*Waterwheels built with an undershot wheel design
rotate as water flows beneath the wheel.*

A waterwheel's power made it possible to perform tasks that
previously had relied on human muscles. Waterwheels could
grind wheat and corn. They could drive machines used for
cleaning wool and spinning thread. Hydropower could provide
energy for a **bellows** that helped keep fires burning. In a process
called hushing, large amounts of water were washed into the
ground to reveal deposits of metals such as tin and gold. In India,
hydropower has historically been used to spin prayer wheels, a
method still in practice today. Prayers are written on the outside
of a wheel and then waterpower rotates them. That frees people
from having to say them out loud.

Hydropower is distinct from solar power, but they are related.
Today, the term "solar power" refers to energy that is captured
directly from the sun. Hydropower comes indirectly from the sun.
All water on earth is recycled. The sun heats water, causing it to
evaporate. The water condenses in clouds, and then falls again as

rain. Energy comes in two forms: Potential energy is the amount of stored energy that can be used. A log of wood or lump of coal has potential energy that is released as heat when it burns. The second form of energy is kinetic. This is energy that is released when something moves. A person running or an apple falling from a tree is demonstrating kinetic energy. Hydropower works by harnessing the kinetic energy of water.

Producing hydropower involves no complicated issues of chemistry or physics. It's just basic mechanics, so the technology was well within the grasp of 19th-century engineers. Although the methods have improved in the last 100 years, the basic idea remains the same. Rushing water is forced into long pipes, called penstocks. Then it's directed onto the blades of a **turbine**. The turbine spins to produce electricity in a generator. The amount of energy provided by water is based on the factors of head and flow. The head is the vertical distance the water falls, while the flow is the amount of water. A "high head" hydropower plant requires less water to produce the same amount of energy because the longer distance the water travels produces more force.

Penstock water pipes are attached to a dam's gate system to control the flow of water.

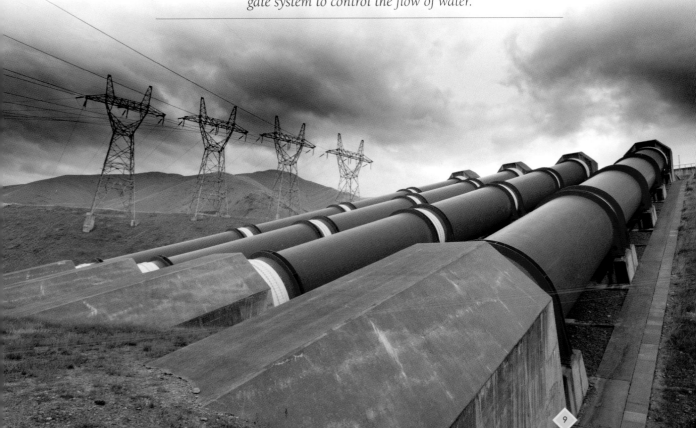

Except in some developing countries, traditional watermills have not operated since the early 1900s.

The amount of electricity that's produced is determined by the amount of water flowing into the plant. The water is controlled by constructing a dam. A dam is essentially a wall. It's usually built high on a river, where it stops the downward flow of water. The water pools behind it to create a **reservoir**. From there, gates can be opened to let water through as needed.

Most large hydroelectric power plants rely on dams, but smaller plants may be "damless," or "run-of-the-river." These plants work with the natural flow of the river's current. The water is simply redirected into pipes and forced through turbines. No water is collected or stored, so it continues along its natural pathway. These types of plants usually generate less power.

At the beginning of the **Industrial Revolution**, many factories depended on waterpower. With the invention of the steam engine, the use of coal began to spread. But the end of the 19th century brought a new technology that would revive hydropower: Electricity became much more widespread. Demand for electricity surged around the turn of the 20th century, and hydropower was there to meet that demand. Hydropower was sometimes called "white coal" because it was a clean, but powerful, energy source.

The world's first hydroelectric plants started operating in the early 1880s. A plant

Hoover Dam, a National Historic Landmark, and Lake Mead attract millions of tourists each year.

built on Niagara Falls in New York in 1881 powered local mills and provided street lighting. In 1882, Wisconsin businessman H. J. Rogers built a small station on the Fox River in Wisconsin. It produced only enough electricity to light the plant itself, Rogers's home, and another building. These small projects showed that hydroelectricity had promise, though. A few years later, a much larger plant came online at Niagara Falls.

Hydropower took off in the 1930s in the United States, thanks to Hoover Dam, on the border of Nevada and Arizona, which was completed in 1936. At the dedication of the dam (then called Boulder Dam), U.S. president Franklin Roosevelt said, "This

morning I came, I saw, and I was conquered, as everyone would be who sees for the first time this great feat of mankind.... [T]he transformation wrought here in these years is a twentieth-century marvel." Six years later, the massive Grand Coulee Dam in Washington state was finished. It was even bigger than the Hoover Dam. There were also several smaller projects. Roosevelt created the Tennessee Valley Authority (TVA) in 1933. That agency assumed the task of building hydroelectric plants along the Mississippi River in the American Southeast, providing jobs and electricity to much of the rural South. The surge in American hydropower came just in time for World War II, which the U.S. was involved in from 1941 to 1945. During this time, brand-new hydropower plants pumped out the electricity needed to make aluminum, a critical material used in building airplanes.

The construction **frenzy** in the U.S. inspired hydro projects all around the world by the 1950s. Hydroelectricity was the one **renewable** source of energy that was economically worth pursuing. Solar and wind technologies were still in their infancy. They were expensive and could not provide much power. Fossil fuels were so cheap that spending money researching renewables didn't seem worth it. Hydro was different, though, since the basic technology already existed. Additionally, people knew it could provide significant amounts of power.

Today, hydropower is used wherever there's enough water. The U.S. and Europe have developed approximately 75 percent of their available spots for large hydroelectric dams. Canada has an extensive infrastructure for hydroelectric power. It's also widely used in South America. The Itaipu Dam on the border of Paraguay and Brazil took 25 years to build and was completed in 1991. Today, it provides almost all of Paraguay's electrical power. There's even some energy left over, which Paraguay is able to sell to Brazil. Large dam sites around the world are getting scarce, but they're not completely exhausted. In 1994, construction started on China's Three Gorges Dam, the largest hydroelectric plant in the world. It reached full capacity in 2012.

After Three Gorges was complete, China announced in 2013 that it would build the world's tallest dam.

CHAPTER TWO

HIGH TIME FOR HYDRO

GINORMOUS. That might be the best word to describe the massive structure that stretches across the Yangtze River in China. The Three Gorges Dam is a supersized example of classic **impoundment** hydropower. In other words, it's a really big dam. Three Gorges is about 600 feet (182 m) tall and almost a mile and a half (2.3 km) across. It's holding back a reservoir that covers 386 square miles (1,000 square km).

The Chinese government expects the dam could replace hundreds of coal-fired electricity plants. It will reduce flooding that happens regularly on the Yangtze. Controlling water flow

According to Chinese media sources, more than 100 workers died during the construction of Three Gorges.

on the dangerous river will improve safety and efficiency for shipping traffic. But the dam comes with a cost that goes beyond money. More than a million people had to move to accommodate the changed course of the river. Hundreds of thousands of acres of farmland disappeared under its waters. Downriver, more farmland may suffer because it will no longer be nourished with **silt** from upstream. Environmental effects such as these make traditional hydro projects controversial. Large dams alter river flows and can disrupt entire ecosystems. In addition, **climate change** is altering the amount of rainfall, which in turn affects how much water is available to run a hydroelectric plant.

Planners hoped Three Gorges would boost trade because of its ability to accommodate large freighters.

One possible solution is to use "pumped storage." These kinds of plants have two reservoirs. Water flows down from an upper reservoir to produce electricity and collects in the lower reservoir. Then it's pumped back up to be used again. Pumped storage helps solve the problem of low river flows. Claude Lambert, president and chief executive officer of the power company Alstom Hydro North America, maintained that pumped storage could be especially useful in places such as the American West, where there is an emphasis on energy conservation and renewables. "[I]t is the most efficient and flexible means of storing energy on a large scale, providing grid stability and enabling a reduction in emissions," Lambert said in 2012.

There are drawbacks to pumped storage, but in many cases the benefits outweigh them. It requires electricity to pump water uphill, and pumped storage plants end up using more energy than they produce. However, they pump when there is low demand for electricity elsewhere. Because electricity is difficult to store, it's a perfect example of the phrase "use it or lose it." The pumping process can use up any extra electricity the plant has produced. In addition, hydro is often ideal for pairing with another source of energy, such as wind. Hydropower can provide electricity to customers during daytime hours. Wind power tends to pick up at night, just when people don't need as much electricity in their homes. At that point, wind can be used to pump water instead.

Countries all over the world rely on hydropower to **supplement** the use of fossil fuels. Not only is hydro renewable, but it's also remarkably efficient. It turns about 90 percent of its energy into useful work, whereas fossil fuels depend on thermal (heat) energy, much of which escapes into the air. Meanwhile, hydroelectricity is more reliable and versatile than other renewables. Because water flows are generally predictable, hydro can produce a reliable amount of electricity for everyday needs. In addition, it's good for "peak" periods, when demand surges. Open the dam gates, let more water through, and the response is almost immediate.

Today, hydropower produces about 16 percent of the world's electricity. Countries such as Albania and Paraguay are national

Thanks to New Zealand's long history of hydropower, it receives half its electricity from the source.

advertisements for hydro. They use it to produce all their electric power. Norway, Iceland, and New Zealand are also big users. But it's the larger countries of the world that make the most overall. Together, China, Canada, Brazil, the U.S., and Russia produce more than half of the world's hydropower. Hydro is the most widely used of all renewable energy sources, and its reach is still expanding. In just one year, 2009 to 2010, global use shot up 5 percent.

Many of the world's obvious sites for large dams have been taken. But one potentially large producer of hydropower still remains: the ocean. The gravitational pull of the moon on the

*Experiments on floating tidal turbines have been
conducted by the Scottish company Scotrenewables.*

earth produces tides, which contain tremendous energy. To
capture this energy, a kind of barrier called a barrage is erected
where the tide comes in. A series of turbines is built into this
wall. The flow of the tide spins turbines that produce electricity.
To work effectively, tidal barrages need about a 16-foot (4.9 m)
difference between high and low tides. Only a handful of places
in the world have tides this large. One is at the Bay of Fundy in
Canada, which has tides up to 50 feet (15.2 m) high! Another
tidal project was ongoing as of 2013 in the East River of New York
City. Turbines there capture the energy under water, so the tides
do not need to be as big.

   Waves are another source of energy. Wave turbines work
much like wind turbines—they are just located underwater.

---

*Energy from rotating underwater turbines travels through
a cable to a generator to produce electricity.*

Coastal areas in the U.S., Europe, and Japan have wave-energy
stations. One common machine used in capturing wave energy is
an **oscillating** water column. First, a large tube of air is inserted
into the water. When a wave hits, it forces the air over a series of
turbines, capturing the energy. In 1974, South African engineer
Stephen Salter invented a system of linked **buoys** that float on
the water. The so-called Salter's ducks bounce on the surface of
the water as waves move them. The resulting energy is captured
and carried onshore through a cable.

Tidal and wave energy technologies have been proven to
work. However, they don't generate much electricity, and they're
expensive. Harnessing the ocean's power also has other problems.
Underwater turbines are loud and potentially disruptive to wildlife.

Also, as energy is drawn out of moving water, the water slows down. If the water runs out of power, it may not reach the place it was originally headed. This could affect marine ecosystems. There's also the danger that sea creatures could get trapped in the equipment and die. Finally, it's difficult and expensive to move electricity over long distances, so ocean energy is still limited to places close to shore.

It's not just motion that provides energy in water. It's also heat. Geothermal energy uses the heat stored inside the earth. Several miles underground is a layer of hot, liquid rock called magma. This magma heats groundwater. Geothermal energy is found all over the world. It's especially accessible where volcanoes are active. The "Ring of Fire" is a string of volcanoes surrounding the Pacific Ocean, from the west coast of the Americas to the east coast of Japan and south to Indonesia, the Philippines, and Hawaii. In places such as these, rumbling volcanoes unsettle the earth, and water can escape. Geysers are plumes of hot water that explode from inside the earth. They are natural examples of geothermal energy. Geothermal energy can be used to heat water for household uses. It's also used to make steam that powers turbines. Geothermal energy is used extensively in Iceland and the Philippines. The U.S. is the world leader in producing electricity from geothermal sources. However, because U.S. demand for electricity is so high, geothermal accounts for only a small percentage of its total energy usage.

Hydropower is struggling to compete with the big boys of fossil fuels. There's only so much water in the world, and it can produce only so much power. Hydropower has virtually no chance of keeping up with the world's increasing demand for electricity. However, with new technologies and different approaches, it can still provide a good portion. It just might need a little makeover first.

The hot baths of Iceland's famous Blue Lagoon were created by the nearby Svartsengi geothermal power station.

CHAPTER THREE

BY LAND OR SEA

HOOVER DAM HAS ISSUES. The water level in its reservoir, Lake Mead, has been steadily falling for years. Some researchers believe that climate changes will only make it worse. In the next decade, Hoover Dam may not have enough water to turn its giant turbines. Such a chain of events is being repeated at dams all over the world. Countries such as Kenya, Venezuela, Peru, Colombia, the Philippines, and China have experienced severe droughts in recent years. This has reduced the flow of their rivers, leading to a decline in hydropower production and electricity shortages. Such circumstances affect how much countries are willing to gamble on getting their electricity from large hydropower plants. Much of China's electricity was

A "bathtub ring" around Lake Mead shows how much water the reservoir has lost in recent years.

Rural residents in Laos construct microhydro systems from readily available materials such as bamboo.

of the amount of electricity of larger plants. But they do not use as much water, so they don't require large sites. There are many smaller sites that can support microhydro. Microhydro is especially attractive in poor or **remote** areas, such as developing nations. People in such areas are often not wired to the **power grid**. They couldn't afford to buy its electricity, even if they were. But a small, local system can provide enough electricity to power a generator that can run lights or appliances. In nations such as Nepal, Ghana, and Peru, rural residents are building microhydro systems.

Future hydropower will likely combine traditional dams with innovative ways of capturing ocean energy from tides and waves.

Tim Fuhr, the director of ocean energy for the American aeronautics company Lockheed Martin, said, "Basically, we see the ocean as the largest untouched source of power on the planet."

One idea for how to tap into that resource is a tidal fence. Unlike a tidal barrage, a fence is not a solid mass—it's a string of underwater turbines. These are cheaper to install, and they do not interfere as much with the environment. In 2008, tidal fences were being discussed for waters off the coast of England and Wales, as well as in the Philippines, but whether those projects will develop further is still to be seen. Another idea is to capture "dynamic tidal power." Some tides don't crash into the shore. Instead, they move parallel to it, out in the ocean. In 1997, two Dutch coastal engineers, Kees Hulsbergen and Rob Steijn, drew up a design for a long, T-shaped dam. The shape of the dam would disrupt the tide and force it through the turbines built into the dam.

Meanwhile, wave-energy technology is growing. A 2011 report from the California-based Electric Power Research Institute estimated that the U.S. could potentially obtain a third of its electricity from waves, if systems were installed along the nation's thousands of miles of coastline. One hurdle to capturing such energy is designing equipment that can stand up to the harsh conditions of the ocean. Sturdy steel turbines and wave buoys can take a beating, but the salty seawater eats away at them over time, and the turbines can break in storms. That means lost power just when things are picking up! Future turbines will be stronger and have fewer moving parts. They will be designed to work even if the water level is lower than expected. They'll also be more "fish-friendly."

Some scientists have figured out how to take advantage of a natural phenomenon called **osmosis**. When seawater and fresh water come together, they naturally mix until the salt level is equal throughout. This happens anywhere a river empties into the sea. However, salty water has a higher pressure, and therefore more potential energy, than fresh water. In 1973, American chemist Sidney Loeb invented a **semipermeable membrane** that divided the two types of water, increasing pressure on one side to produce energy. Systems modeled on Loeb's membrane were being developed in Norway and the Netherlands in the early 2010s.

Another type of ocean energy is called Ocean Thermal Energy Conversion (OTEC). It takes advantage of the temperature difference between cold water deep in the ocean and warmer water near the surface. OTEC systems work best in tropical climates, where the temperature difference is the greatest. A substance with a low boiling point, such as ammonia or propane,

Rising oil prices have recently prompted companies to develop innovative designs for OTEC projects.

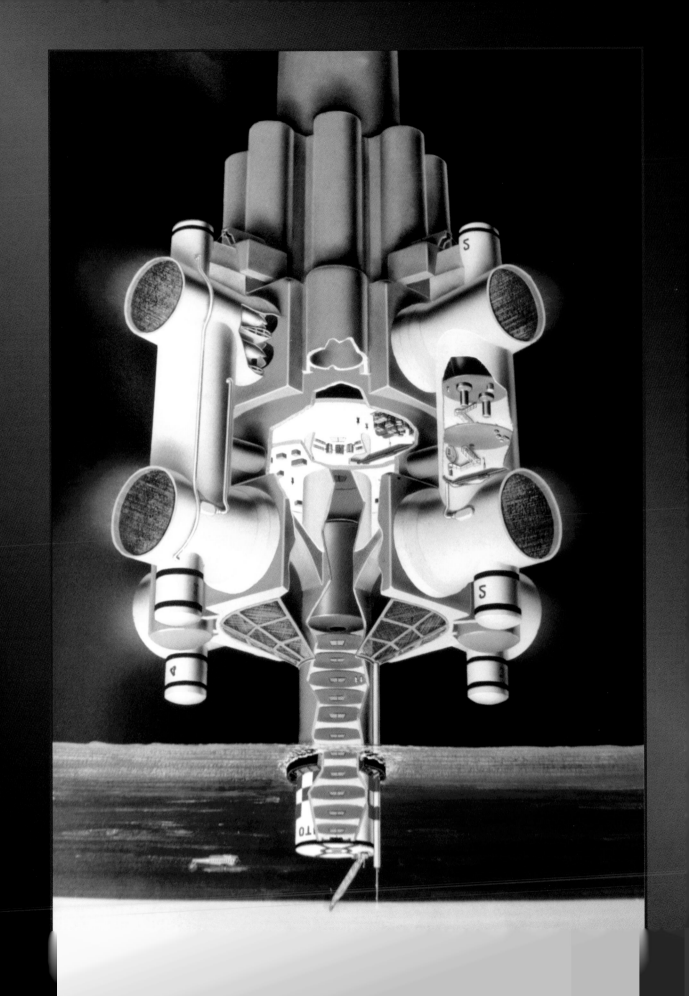

is put into a long loop of underwater pipe. At the top of the loop, warm ocean water boils the substance. It turns to gas and expands. The pressure pushes turbines to produce electricity. Then the gas travels through the loop down to the cooler ocean water, where it compresses back into a liquid, and the cycle starts again. Scientists are working to build systems that will be efficient even if the temperature difference is small.

Geothermal energy is also heating up.

Since the 1970s, research has been underway in the U.S., Japan, Australia, and Europe. Turkey, Kenya, and Indonesia are also actively growing this resource. The research firm GlobalData projected worldwide use to double between 2008 and 2015. In 2007, researchers at the Massachusetts Institute of Technology concluded that the U.S. had significant opportunities for producing electricity from geothermal energy. In their report, they concluded, "By almost any criteria, the accessible U.S. [geothermal] resource base is enormous … 130,000 times the current annual consumption of primary energy in the United States." They went on to note that, while the actual amount recovered would be much lower, none of the technical hurdles was insurmountable.

The International Energy Agency (IEA) has predicted that electricity generation from renewable energy sources, including hydro, solar, and wind power, will roughly triple from 2009 to 2035. Several factors would drive that growth, including improvements in technology and increased political support at the government level. Both of those factors help cut costs for renewable-source power generation. This could be good news for hydropower, especially for smaller projects and "alternative" hydro systems that use geothermal and ocean energy.

CHAPTER FOUR

STAYING AFLOAT

IN ONE VERSION OF THE LEGEND OF ATLANTIS, RECOUNTED BY THE GREEK PHILOSOPHER PLATO, AN ANCIENT CIVILIZATION OF WARRIORS LIVED ON AN ISLAND IN THE ATLANTIC OCEAN. After failing to conquer the Greek city-state of Athens, in Greece, Atlantis sank into the ocean—or was somehow swallowed up by it—and was never seen again. Today, communities all over the world have faced a similar but much less mysterious fate. The battle to provide electricity has meant the construction of dams whose reservoirs often flood adjacent towns. People's homes, stores, farms, and history became buried under thousands of feet of water. In Canada, which has a long history of hydro, thousands of people have been uprooted. Projects in South America, Africa, and Asia also threaten to displace native populations. More than one million people lost their homes to the Three Gorges Dam in China.

The Chinese tried to protect culturally important sites such as the city of Fengdu from projected rising waters.

After a dam is built, new problems often arise. A 2010
report from the Nature Conservancy concluded that dams had
negatively affected about 472 million people worldwide, through
displacement or by altering the land they depend on. Reduced river
flow downstream can affect fishers or other people who depend
on the river to make their living. Upstream, danger lurks behind
the walls of a dam. If one breaks, it unleashes millions of gallons
of water that can flood a town, killing people and destroying
property. These disasters, while uncommon, are often sudden
and unexpected. Three Gorges was built in an area susceptible to

High-water markers along riverbanks help to
track the flooding levels caused by dams.

earthquakes. Two Chinese civil engineers, Li Ping and Li Yuanjun, warned that "a medium or strong earthquake would set off a chain of events in the reservoir area, with a series of landslides and riverbank collapses being triggered.... The consequences could be dreadful to **contemplate**, quite unimaginable."

People may be warned when a hydroelectric project is planned, but plants and animals often suffer great consequences as well. Large hydropower projects can cause long-term damage to ecosystems. Running water is typically cooler than a still reservoir. Some species can't take the heat, while others are ill-equipped to live in confined spaces. Some fish, such as salmon, require a free-flowing river, because they swim upstream to get to their breeding grounds. In the U.S., dams on the Columbia and Snake Rivers in the Pacific

*Activists and residents sometimes protest dam construction
and its effects on industries such as fishing.*

Northwest have **depleted** fish populations, and on the East Coast,
salmon are endangered by dams on the Kennebec and Androscoggin
Rivers in Maine. China's Three Gorges Dam possibly wiped out
the Yangtze River dolphin, a species of freshwater dolphin that
is thought to be extinct. Also, dammed rivers do not contain as
much water downstream. Hoover Dam blocked the Colorado River
from flowing freely south into Mexico. Historically, the river had
nourished a Mexican jungle hundreds of miles to the south. After the
dam was built, the area withered from lack of water.

Alternative hydro technologies can be controversial, too.
Fishers and surfers sometimes oppose wave and tidal turbines
because they get in their way. Geothermal makes other people
nervous. Most of the earth's heat is far underground. Drilling
to reach it can trigger earthquakes, especially since many of the

world's best geothermal resources are found in areas that are already susceptible to earthquakes. In 2006, a geothermal drilling operation in Switzerland set off a 3.4 magnitude earthquake, while a project in California called the Geysers has routinely been causing small earthquakes. Geothermal energy is accessed by fracturing rocks. However, if the size of the fractures is kept small, it reduces the chance of earthquakes.

Advocates of hydropower love to point out that it's clean. It doesn't spew poisonous chemicals into the air and soil as fossil fuels do. However, it does produce the greenhouse gas methane. Fossil fuels make greenhouse gases such as carbon dioxide when they burn, but methane is about 20 times worse. Hydroelectric plants can be big methane-makers. When a river is dammed, it creates a reservoir that buries all the vegetation that used to grow there. As these plants die and decay, they produce methane. When the reservoir depletes, new plants grow, but then they die when the water level rises again, producing more methane. Éric Duchemin, a consultant for the Intergovernmental Panel on Climate Change (IPCC), warned that few people consider this environmental effect. In an interview in 2005 for *New Scientist* magazine, Duchemin said, "Everyone thinks hydro is very clean, but this is not the case."

Concerns such as these can slow the progress of new hydropower projects. In Tibet, water at the "Great Bend" in the Brahmaputra River provides tremendous force as it flows from the Himalayan Mountains into the lower regions of India and Nepal. However, no major hydro project has been built there so far. The engineering challenges it poses are huge, and the environmental impact could be even greater. Also, if the river's flow of water to India is disrupted, it could put India at an economic and political disadvantage to China. Similar battles over water rights rage throughout the region and in naturally drier areas such as northern Africa. A project underway in Ethiopia threatens to cut water supplies to Egypt and Sudan.

The Belo Monte dam, on Brazil's Xingu River, is also controversial. It will significantly impact the Amazon rainforest and displace **indigenous** peoples. The project has been on and off for

In 2012, people being displaced by the Belo Monte dam removed an earthen section of it in protest.

years as the government and environmentalists battle over whether it should proceed. Still, the Brazilian government was enthusiastic about building new hydro plants and had plans to construct about 20 more by the early 2020s. The country has excellent river sources to support such power and already gets almost 90 percent of its electricity through hydro. Demand for electricity is expected to increase by more than 50 percent by 2021, but if Brazil can continue to manufacture its electricity with hydro, it will be able to stay away from fossil fuels.

Reducing fossil-fuel dependence would be a good step toward achieving "energy security." Many countries want to be independent when it comes to energy. Then, they do not have to rely on imported fuels from other countries.

Using a **domestic** source of energy frees them up from having to negotiate on the price or potentially losing a supply of energy because of political conflicts. Domestic energy sources also tend to be cheaper because of reduced transportation costs.

Studies have shown that increased access to electricity can improve the standard of living and even help people live longer. However, billions of people worldwide have little or no electricity. Because of where they live, hydropower might be their best bet of obtaining greater access to energy—and the comforts that come with electricity. A video produced by the African Development Bank (AfDB) promised that, "If one day the Inga dam rises up the River Congo, the entire

African economy will rise with it." Such sweeping change seems unrealistic, though. It has been shown that large hydro systems do not always benefit rural residents in developing countries. Many people report that these projects take away their water without supplying much electricity in return. Instead, it is piped away to large cities.

Renewable energy, including hydropower, is still more expensive than fossil fuels. That could change, however. As fossil fuels become harder to find and extract, their prices will increase. And many people are concerned about the environmental "costs" fossil fuels entail. National governments all over the world are cracking down on the pollution caused by fossil fuels. They are requiring companies that use fossil fuels to either cut back or pay more. Such measures could eventually raise the end cost to consumers and make renewables look more attractive.

Rain falls, rivers flow to the sea, tides go in and out. Water itself may be enduring, but its patterns don't stay the same. The polar ice caps are melting, rivers are drying up, and coastal areas are flooding. Some areas get too much rain, and others get too little. Water is all over—it just comes in different forms. People have been nipping and tucking at the earth's water for thousands of years, and that's not likely to change. They may just have to change how they do it.

Hydropower project supporters hope to control rising waters and prevent global flooding.

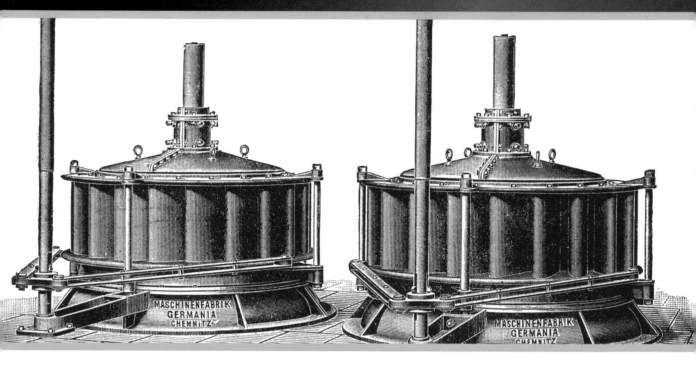

Sometimes it's necessary to look inward, not out. That's what British-American engineer James Francis did. In 1849, Francis was living in Lowell, Massachusetts, an industrial town that depended heavily on hydropower. Francis invented a new kind of inward-flow water turbine that improved its efficiency to more than 90 percent. Inward-flow turbines allow water to swirl to the center. The energy of the moving water turns a shaft that then powers a generator. Francis turbines are versatile and are still used more than any other type. They produce about 60 percent of the world's hydropower.

French science fiction author Jules Verne introduced the concept of Ocean Thermal Energy Conversion (OTEC) in the mid-1800s. Scientists wondered if it could really work. The idea depended on the transfer of heat between warmer and cooler water that happens naturally in the ocean. By 1928, French engineer Georges Claude had successfully tested a system in Belgium. Next he headed to the tropical region of Matanzas, Cuba, where he built an OTEC plant in 1930. He built another one in Brazil in 1935. Both stations were later destroyed in storms, but Claude had proved the technology could work.

Francis's invention (above) improved upon the waterwheels and turbines of the past and is used today for both electricity production and pumped storage in reservoirs.

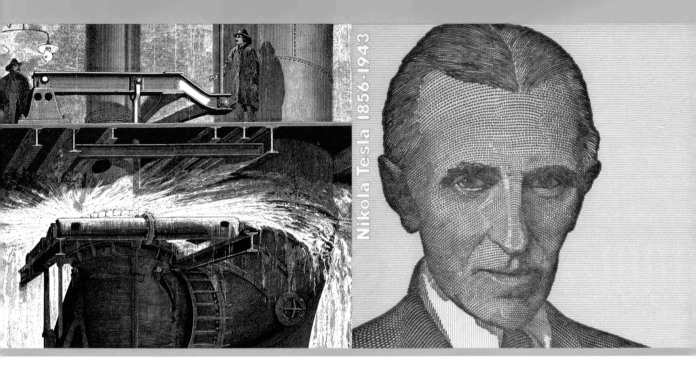

As a boy, Croatian scientist and inventor Nikola Tesla wanted to harness the power of Niagara Falls using a wheel. In 1895, Tesla and American inventor George Westinghouse built a hydroelectric plant for the Falls, which are located between the U.S. and Canada. The innovative plant would produce electricity using the technology of alternating current, instead of direct current, as a means of enabling the electricity to travel farther. In 1896, the plant delivered electricity to Buffalo, New York, about 26 miles (40 km) away. Alternating current hydroelectric power had been used to move electricity long distances in Europe before, but it was a first for North America.

They called it the "iron dam." When China's ten-year-old Banqiao Dam first showed signs of cracking in the 1960s, engineers repaired it in a way they thought would be unbreakable. They were wrong. In the summer of 1975, Typhoon Nina brought more rain in one day than the area normally got in an entire year. As the waters rose, a smaller dam broke upstream. Half an hour later, so did Banqiao. Before the disaster was over, 62 dams in the hydroelectric network had failed, knocking out power to millions. Floods killed about 26,000 people, and another 145,000 later died from hunger or disease. It was the most catastrophic dam failure in history.

The plant success at Niagara (left) contributed to the "War of Currents," a competition engaged in by Westinghouse and Tesla (right) against inventor Thomas Edison.

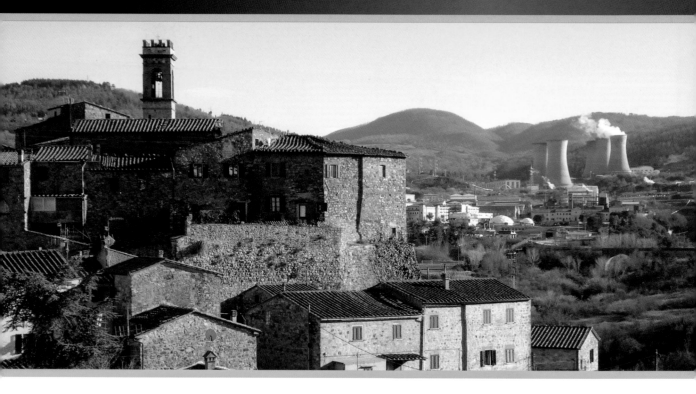

Geothermal energy has been hot in Italy since the days of ancient Rome, when people would bathe in the natural hot springs. In 1904, geothermal energy was first used to produce electricity in Italy. Steam rising from vents in the earth powered a turbine that lit up five light bulbs. In 1913, a power plant in Larderello, called "Devil's Valley," became the world's first geothermal power station. It provided power to run the country's electric railroad. Today, it provides electricity to about one million homes. However, the pressure of the erupting steam has dropped about 30 percent since the 1950s, so it may not prove to be **sustainable**.

In 1997, people from 20 countries came together in Curitiba, Brazil, for the First International Meeting of People Affected by Dams. They represented the millions who had been negatively affected by large hydroelectric projects. Some had lost their homes. Others depended on river flow to make their living. After the meeting, a group called the World Commission on Dams was formed. In 2000, the members of this group issued a report about how future hydroelectric dams should be built to balance power needs with the rights of people who lived near proposed dam sites.

For decades, Devil's Valley, nicknamed for the Italian region's boiling water and rising steam, was the only industrial producer of geothermal energy in the world (above).

Tides are reliable, which is a good thing, considering it took more than 40 years to make the idea of building a tidal power plant in France a reality. The 26-foot (8 m) tides on the Rance River were still there in 1966, when the world's first tidal power plant opened. It was connected to the country's national power grid the following year. The tidal barrage is 2,461 feet long (750 m) and generates enough electricity yearly for about 300,000 people. In 1997, the plant was upgraded with turbines that spin in two directions, producing electricity both when the tide comes in and when it goes out.

All eyes were on a single light bulb. About 150 villagers in rural Nepal waited to see if it would light up. When it did, they cheered. The bulb was powered with electricity generated from a microhydro project that was built in 2001. Many Nepalese citizens live in areas that are too remote to be connected to an electric grid. Nepal's powerful rivers make it ideal for small, run-of-the-river plants that do not require a dam. Electricity has cut down on the amount of tough, physical work that residents have to do, and incomes have risen as a result.

France's tidal plant needed two dams in order to drain the construction area (left).
Microhydro projects can have big effects on a country's overall energy outlook (right).

GLOSSARY

bellows—a device used to pump air

buoy—a device designed to float

climate change—a phenomenon in which weather patterns undergo significant and long-term changes

contemplate—to consider, ponder

deplete—to lessen in amount

domestic—within any given nation; not involving other countries

fossil fuels—fuels formed by decaying plants and animals over millions of years

frenzy—intense activity

global warming—the phenomenon of Earth's average temperatures increasing over time

greenhouse gases—gases that build up in Earth's atmosphere and prevent the release of heat

impoundment—a state of being contained or confined

indigenous—native to an area

Industrial Revolution—a period from the late 1700s through the 1800s in Europe and the U.S. marked by a shift from economies based on agriculture and handicraft to ones dominated by mechanized production in factories

oscillating—moving back and forth steadily, like a pendulum

osmosis—a process by which two different substances mix until their properties are the same

power grid—a system for distributing power throughout a community

remote—distant, isolated

renewable—able to be replenished and used indefinitely

reservoir—a large body of water collected for use at a later time

semipermeable membrane—a thin, filmy barrier that is partially penetrable by a gas or liquid

silt—fine dirt or sediment that is carried by running water

supplement—to provide additional resources, make up for a lack of something

sustainable—able to be maintained over a long period

turbine—a machine that is driven by water, steam, or a gas flowing through the blades of a wheel

Charlier, Roger H., and Charles W. Finkl. *Ocean Energy: Tide and Tidal Power*. Berlin: Springer-Verlag, 2009.

Craddock, David. *Renewable Energy Made Easy: Free Energy from Solar, Wind, Hydropower, and Other Alternative Energy Sources*. Ocala, Fla.: Atlantic Publishing Group, 2008.

Galbraith, Kate. "Hydropower's Resurgence and the Controversy Around It." *New York Times*, May 15, 2011.

Koerth-Baker, Maggie. *Before the Lights Go Out: Conquering the Energy Crisis before It Conquers Us*. Hoboken, N.J.: Wiley, 2012.

Liu, Coco, and ClimateWire. "Climate Change Evaporates Part of China's Hydropower." ScientificAmerican.com. November 8, 2011. http://www.scientificamerican.com/article.cfm?id=climate-change-evaporates-china-hydropower-production-drop-25-percent&page=2.

National Energy Education Development Project. *Secondary Energy Infobook*. Manassas, Vir.: The NEED Project, 2012.

Vee, Amy. "Microhydro Drives Change in Rural Nepal." *New York Times*, June 20, 2012.

Woody, Todd. "The Next Wave in Renewable Energy." *Forbes*, February 27, 2012.

Worldwatch Institute. "Use and Capacity of Global Hydropower Increases." WorldWatch.org. January 17, 2012. http://www.worldwatch.org/use-and-capacity-global-hydropower-increases.

Land Art Generator Initiative

http://landartgenerator.org/readwater.html

In its mission to encourage the construction of artistic structures for renewable energy generation, this website provides a good overview of different technologies for hydro, solar, and wind power.

U.S. Energy Information Administration

http://www.eia.gov/kids/energy.cfm?page=hydropower_home-basics

This section of the U.S. Energy Information Administration's website provides information on hydropower's history, how it works, and where it's used.

NOTE: *Every effort has been made to ensure that the websites listed above are suitable for children, that they have educational value, and that they contain no inappropriate material. However, because of the nature of the Internet, it is impossible to guarantee that these sites will remain active indefinitely or that their contents will not be altered.*

Barker, Geoff. *Water*. Mankato, Minn.: Smart Apple Media, 2010.

Bodden, Valerie. *Water for Life*. Mankato, Minn.: Creative Education, 2011.

Gunderson, Jessica. *The Energy Dilemma*. Mankato, Minn.: Creative Education, 2011.

Morris, Neil. *Water Power*. Mankato, Minn.: Smart Apple Media, 2010.

Oxlade, Chris. *Energy Technology*. Mankato, Minn.: Smart Apple Media, 2012.

Royston, Angela. *Sustainable Energy*. Mankato, Minn.: Arcturus, 2009.

Solway, Andrew. *Climate Change*. Mankato, Minn.: Smart Apple Media, 2010.

Published by Creative Paperbacks
P.O. Box 227, Mankato, Minnesota 56002
Creative Paperbacks is an imprint of The Creative Company
www.thecreativecompany.us

Design and production by The Design Lab
Art direction by Rita Marshall
Printed in the United States of America

Photographs by Alamy (Arcaid Images, James Caldwell, DBA Images, epa european
pressphoto agency b.v., INTERFOTO, Steve Morgan), Corbis (Yann Arthus-Bertrand,
Cheng Min/Xinhua Press, Qiu Shafeng/epa), Dreamstime (Danielsnaer, Martin Darley,
Drimi, Gan Hui, Georgios Kollidas, Prabindai, Karolina Vyskocilova), Getty Images
(Van D Bucher, Mario Tama), Shutterstock (Denis Barbulat, Sissy Borbely, Alexandru
Chiriac, Mark Dumbleton, Eddie_, Johann Helgason, Ifelix, Martin Lehmann, Miks,
Alex Mit, Pi-Lens, rook76, Irina Schmidt, Videowokart, Narongsak Yaisumlee)

Library of Congress Cataloging-in-Publication Data
Bailey, Diane.
Hydropower / Diane Bailey.
p. cm. — (Harnessing energy)
Includes bibliographical references and index.
Summary: An examination of the ways in which water has historically been
used as an energy source and how current and future energy demands
are changing its technical applications and efficiency levels.
ISBN 978-1-60818-410-1 (hardcover)
ISBN 978-0-89812-996-0 (pbk)
1. Hydroelectric power plants—Juvenile literature.
2. Water-power—Juvenile literature. I. Title.

TK1081.B275 2014
621.31'2134—dc23   2013035753

CCSS: RI.5.1, 2, 3, 4, 8, 9

First Edition
9 8 7 6 5 4 3 2 1